LANGSTON HUGHES
Poet of His People

LANGSTON HUGHES

POET OF HIS PEOPLE

by Elisabeth P. Myers

illustrated by Russell Hoover

GARRARD PUBLISHING COMPANY
CHAMPAIGN, ILLINOIS

Acknowledgments

Excerpts on pages 23, 39, 46, 50, 52, 87, 90 (both) reprinted
from *The Big Sea* by Langston Hughes, © copyright 1940
by Langston Hughes.

Excerpts on pages 115, 125, 126 reprinted from *I Wonder As I Wander*
by Langston Hughes, © copyright 1956 by Langston Hughes.

Excerpt on page 133 reprinted from page 122 of *The Best of Simple*
by Langston Hughes.

> All of the above by permission of the publisher,
> Hill & Wang, Inc.

Poems by Langston Hughes on pages 60, 64, 81 (both), 86, 88, 106,
110, 118, 129, 130, 134 reprinted from *Selected Poems* by Langston
Hughes, © copyright 1959 by Langston Hughes.

Poems by Langston Hughes on pages 73 and 103 reprinted from *The Dream
Keeper* by Langston Hughes, (copyright 1932 and renewed 1960 by Langston
Hughes).

Five lines from "Poem" by Langston Hughes on page 106 reprinted from
The Weary Blues by Langston Hughes, copyright 1926 by Alfred A. Knopf,
Inc. (renewed 1954 by Langston Hughes).

> All of the above by permission of the publisher,
> Alfred A. Knopf, Inc.

Picture credits:

Roy De Carava: p. 2-3, 127, 128, 132, 137, 138
Dodat, Francois, *Langston Hughes* (Paris: Editions Seghers, 1964): p. 43, 96, 121
Schomburg Collection, New York Public Library: p. 76, 79, 93, 102, 105, 108, 140
United Press International: p. 118

Contents

1. Earthquake!

One April afternoon in 1907, five-year-old Langston Hughes sat in a train crossing Mexico. He was tired and cross and fidgety, because he and his mother and his grandmother had been traveling for three days. He wasn't even interested in looking out the window any more. All he wanted was to reach their destination — Mexico City — and to hurry at once to the ranch his father owned in the countryside beyond.

"Will my father have a pony for me, do you think?" Langston wondered aloud.

His grandmother, Mrs. Mary Leary Langston, shrugged her shoulders. "Well, knowing James Hughes, I doubt it," she said.

"But Lang doesn't know James," his mother retorted.

And it was true, he didn't. James Hughes had left home for Mexico when Langston was still a baby.

"A Negro is better appreciated outside the United States than in it," he had said. "So I'm going outside to live."

Langston's mother hadn't gone with her husband, because she kept expecting him to change his mind. He didn't, and from time to time he had written, asking her to join him. Finally she had decided to try his way of life.

"Will he?" asked Langston again. "Will he have a pony for me, Ma?"

"I don't know, Lang," said Mrs. Hughes. "He has horses and lots of land. So—maybe."

Even the "maybe" satisfied Langston. He hugged himself and hummed excitedly.

His grandmother frowned. "You're giving the boy false hopes," she warned.

Before Mrs. Hughes could reply, the locomotive whistled and the train slowed.

"See if you can spot your father," she said to Langston instead.

He pressed his nose against the window, looking for a man in a cowboy hat amid the crowd in Mexican *sombreros* and regular city clothes.

The man who greeted his mother with a kiss didn't look a bit like Langston's idea of a rancher. He wore a round derby hat and had a short bristly mustache like a toothbrush.

Langston shrank away from him in disappointment.

"You bringing up a shy boy, Carrie?" Mr. Hughes asked his wife accusingly.

"He's not usually shy," she replied, and pushed him forward. "Kiss your father, Lang."

Langston put up his face and was tickled by his father's mustache.

"When are we going to the ranch?" he asked.

"Tomorrow," said James Hughes. He turned to his wife. "I thought you'd probably had enough traveling for today."

"I'm sure Lang has," she answered. "He needs a chance to stretch his legs."

Across from the hotel was a park with tiled paths and spouting fountains. After dinner, Langston and his parents went for a walk there. Suddenly, Langston let go of their hands and raced ahead. He skidded to a stop by a fountain and stooped down to dabble in the water.

His father strode after him and jerked him upright. "No son of mine is going to act like a street urchin!" he said.

Langston looked in bewilderment at his mother. Her lips were set in a firm line, and her eyes were blazing, but she said nothing. When Langston took her hand again, she squeezed it. He held on tightly for the rest of the walk, but he was glad when it was time to go to bed.

Around midnight, Langston was awakened by a loud crackling. His bed was shaking and a picture came crashing to the floor. He was trembling with fear when his father rushed in and snatched him out of bed.

"Earthquake!" James Hughes said, and ran with Langston out of the hotel and across to the park.

In his fright, Langston didn't remember his earlier scolding. He was too glad to be held securely in his father's arms. All about them people were on their knees praying or shaking their fists at the heavens and swearing, as on every side of the park, buildings toppled like piles of toy blocks. The noise was terrible.

The next morning, the city seemed to be in ruins. Carrie Hughes decided to take the act of God as a warning.

"You and I aren't meant to be together," she told her husband. "I guessed it five years ago, when I refused to come here with you. I don't know why I thought anything was changed now."

"So what are you going to do? Go back again to your mother's house in Kansas and forget that I exist again?" James Hughes said heatedly. "Well, believe me, this time I won't let you forget."

"What do you mean?" she asked.

Her voice was so quavery that Langston, who had been only half listening, now waited for the answer too.

"Because something has changed," his father said. "Langston's not a mound of baby clothes any longer, but a boy. A *Negro* boy. I won't let you ruin his life. He's going to have the same chance to get ahead I've had, only sooner."

Carrie Hughes reached out for Langston and hugged him to her. "You wouldn't keep him here!" she cried.

"Not yet. He'd still be too much trouble. But when I do send for him, you'd better see he comes. You hear me?"

She drew a deep, shuddering sigh. "I hear," she said.

Langston heard too, but he didn't like what he heard. He began to cry.

"You promised I was going to the ranch today!" he sobbed.

"Stop that sniffling," his father said.

Langston hiccoughed, but he tried to control his tears.

James Hughes looked pleased. He pulled out a big handkerchief and wiped Langston's nose.

Langston felt his mother stiffen. "We're going back to Kansas as soon as we can get a train," she said. "I don't want to hear another word about that ranch."

Mrs. Langston, after hearing the story, spoke soothingly to her grandson. "Just think how cozy it will be in your own little room up under the eaves," she said, referring to Langston's bedroom in her home in Lawrence, Kansas.

Langston, remembering how frightening the past night had been, was comforted. Besides, her words reminded him of something else pleasant. Mrs. Langston's house was near the campus of the University of Kansas. Sometimes she rented rooms to students.

"Will you get some college boys to live with us?" he asked. "I like to hear them talk!"

Mrs. Langston chuckled. "*And* to imitate them," she said. "I declare to goodness, you use more big words than any other youngster I *ever* heard."

"Well, will you?" Langston persisted.

"I'll try," she promised.

With that prospect ahead of him, Langston didn't complain again about not seeing the ranch. He didn't even turn around to wave good-bye to his father from the train, until his grandmother prompted him.

2. When You Feel Like Crying, Laugh

Langston was again doomed to disappointment in Kansas. The college term was almost over and students were not looking for housing.

"I wish we'd never gone to Mexico," he complained.

"You hush about that," his grandmother told him.

"Well, don't *you* miss having the boys around?" Langston said.

"Yes," Mrs. Langston admitted, "but not for the reason you do."

She didn't explain, but later Langston found out why.

"Another payment on the house is due," she said to Langston's mother. "Without rent coming in, I don't know how I can ever meet it."

Carrie Hughes sighed. "The amount of money I can make in this town barely pays Lang's and my share, I know. I'm a good typist, but there are too many young faculty wives who are just as good. Since they're white, they get first choice at jobs, even though I've had as much education as they have. Sometimes I think Jimmy was right, going off to Mexico like he did."

"Shame on you," Mrs. Langston said. "Running away instead of fighting isn't *ever* right. It's no kind of example to set for Langston, either."

"Well, he's got to learn sooner or later that being a Negro isn't easy," Mrs. Hughes replied.

"Of course he does," said Mrs. Langston, "but at the same time, he should learn to be proud that he is black."

That afternoon Langston was sitting beside his grandmother's rocking chair. She was reading her Bible while he played with the wooden animals a family friend, whom he called Uncle

Reed, had whittled for him. He wished she'd tell him a story, or read him one.

Finally he asked, "Will you read me about Noah's ark, Gran? From where it says 'God saw that the wickedness of man was great upon the earth . . .'" He rolled the words over his tongue.

Mrs. Langston chuckled. "How you do relish sounds!"

She opened her Bible to the familiar story, but when she came to the words Langston had quoted, she stopped.

Langston tugged at her skirt. "Go on, Gran!" he said.

But she closed the book and set it aside. "Not about Noah," she said. "Instead, I'm going to tell you a story about something the 'wickedness of man' brings to mind."

Langston liked his grandmother's "remembering" stories even better than Bible stories. He put down his animals and climbed into her lap. She settled him comfortably against her, rocked for a moment, and then began to speak.

"Not so long ago," she said, "many Negroes in the states south of Kansas were not free to come and go as they pleased. Rich white people owned them the way — well, the way you do those wooden animals of yours. And those white people made their Negroes — they were called slaves — do what they wanted them to do, just as you do your toys."

Langston squirmed. "That doesn't seem fair," he said. "People aren't toys."

"That's what a lot of people in the North thought," Mrs. Langston continued. "Among them was a white man here in Kansas named John Brown. He was sure he'd heard God's voice telling him to destroy slavery in any way he could. So he called for brave men to go South and help him. Eighteen men volunteered — thirteen white men and five Negroes. One of the Negroes was my first husband, Sheridan Leary."

"What happened to them?" asked Langston.

"John Brown was killed for trying to obey God's voice. So was Sheridan Leary. But their deaths made a lot of Northerners angry, and as soon as enough of them were mad enough, they started fighting the white Southerners. That fight was called the 'Civil War,' up here in the North."

"Was everybody free, after the Civil War was over?" asked Langston.

"According to the law of the land, yes," said his grandmother. "But a lot of white people didn't want to obey that law. They acted like it wasn't so. And that's why my second husband — your Grandfather Langston — did what he could to convince them. He went into politics and made speeches. So did your great uncle, Congressman John Mercer Langston. *He* was so good, President Rutherford Hayes appointed him United States consul general to Haiti!"

Langston didn't know what "consul general" meant, but he could tell from his grandmother's voice that it was something to be proud about.

"I guess that was a pretty important thing to be, wasn't it, Gran?" he asked.

"It was, and don't you ever forget it, honey.

You come from a long line of Negro men who didn't spend any time crying about what was wrong. They set about trying to make things *right*."

"I don't cry much," said Langston.

His grandmother sighed. "Praise God, you haven't had much reason to, yet. But I'm telling you now, boy, don't *ever*. When you feel like crying, laugh instead."

Mrs. Langston's wise advice had a way of sticking with people—even Langston's mother. She went to the state capital, Topeka, where she might find a better job. There she found a position as private secretary to a prominent Negro attorney. Then she returned to get Langston.

"Now you can rent the whole house and live with your friends the Reeds awhile," Carrie Hughes told her mother. "They're always asking you."

Langston was lonesome in Topeka until the day his mother took him to visit the public library. There in the children's room he discovered that books were not just for big people. They

were for him too. Years later, when he wrote the story of his life, he said:

> "There I first fell in love with librarians
> —those very nice women who help you
> find wonderful books. And right then
> and there, before I was six, books
> began to happen to me . . ."

He found the library a peaceful place, too, and after he entered school he was often glad to have it as a place for escape. As the only Negro in an all white school, he was sometimes called names and "picked on" by a few of the other children. But he remembered his grandmother's warning, and though he couldn't always manage to laugh when he felt bad, he didn't cry, either.

When his mother saw how much Langston enjoyed books, she took him to the theater. He loved this new enlarged world of make-believe.

But then, just as suddenly as she had taken him away, his mother returned him to Lawrence and to his grandmother.

"I've decided to divorce Jimmy," Mrs. Hughes told Mrs. Langston. "May Langston stay with you while I'm gone?"

Lawrence seemed very dull to Langston after Topeka. He kept hoping his mother would come back for him soon.

She didn't come back, but got a job in Denver. Children weren't allowed where she lived, she said. So Langston stayed in Lawrence and went to school.

When he was twelve years old, his grandmother died. At her funeral, he remained dry eyed. People scolded him for being a "heartless child," and he looked at them reproachfully.

"Gran told me, 'Don't ever cry,'" he replied. "'When you feel like crying, laugh instead,' she said."

Only his grandmother's best friends, the Reeds, seemed to understand.

3. The Salt of the Earth

Langston went to live with the Reeds after the funeral. They were not educated people like his mother and grandmother, who had both attended college. But Langston soon learned why his Bible-reading Grandmother had called them "the salt of the earth." They were folksy people, warm and lovable. Auntie Reed was a church-goer and delighted in singing spirituals. Uncle Reed "never darkened the door of a church," as he said, but he lived according to the Golden Rule anyhow.

Langston was happy in the Reeds' easy-going household. Uncle Reed had a steady job digging ditches and laying sewer pipes for the city.

Auntie Reed kept a cow and some chickens and a little vegetable patch.

Both of them insisted that Langston keep on going to school, because they knew how much his grandmother wanted him to be educated.

"We've got enough to keep body and soul together for the three of us," they said. "If you want spending money, you can work at something in your playtime."

Langston liked the idea of getting a job. Maybe he could make enough money so he could go to the movies! He had never forgotten the wonderful year he had spent in Topeka, when he and his mother had seen all the plays in town. During the years since, he had not once attended a theater. His grandmother could not afford tickets.

The only job he knew about was delivering papers door to door. He found a paper dealer who was willing to give him a route, and for a while he covered it faithfully. But it was hard to collect money from his customers, and the paper dealer took a large percentage of the small sum he managed to get. It was discouraging.

Finally, he complained to Uncle Reed. "I work hard," he said, "but sometimes I don't have two nickels to rub together at the end of the week."

"Don't hardly seem worthwhile," Uncle Reed sympathized. "Want me to keep my ear to the ground for a better job for you?"

Langston hesitated. The kind of work Uncle Reed would hear about wasn't likely to be the sort his grandmother would have approved. Even when she needed money most, she wouldn't do what she called "demeaning" work, like washing and ironing other people's clothes or cleaning their houses.

"Well?" said Uncle Reed. "Do you or don't you?"

Langston made up his mind. He wanted money more than he wanted to keep his hands clean. "I do," he said.

In a few days, Uncle Reed told him about a job in a nearby hotel. "Won't be pretty work," he warned, "but you'll get paid regular."

"That's what counts," said Langston.

He had to remind himself of that often, for the

work certainly was not "pretty." He had to clean the lobby and the lavatories. He had to shine the mirrors, polish the brass spittoons, and scrub the worn floors on his hands and knees. But he was paid 50 cents a week, and that was enough for a ticket to the movies.

Every Saturday afternoon for months, Langston saw a different movie and all the great movie stars of the time. Then one day he went up to buy a ticket as usual, and the ticket seller refused to sell him one.

"Can't you read?" she asked, and nodded toward a new sign on the wall behind her.

It said: NO COLORED ADMITTED.

Langston was stunned. "But—but that's not fair!" he sputtered. "My money's as good as anybody else's. Besides, I've been coming here for weeks!"

"Sorry," she said, but she didn't sound a bit sorry to Langston.

He continued to stand where he was, until the ticket seller spoke sharply to him. "You going to move, or shall I call the manager?"

Trembling all over with deep resentment and disbelief, Langston stepped out of line and made his way slowly down the street.

"It's not right," he said to himself, over and over. He began to understand what his grandmother had meant by saying that Negroes still had to convince white people that the Civil War was over. Maybe his father *hadn't* been too far wrong to move to Mexico, because he wanted to live where he could be treated equally!

Fortunately for Langston, the Reeds belittled

his experience. "Won't do you a bit of good to cry over spilt milk," they told him. "Just tell yourself, things will be better tomorrow or the next day."

Uncle Reed was soon proved right about the "day after," for Langston discovered the road shows that were staged in the opera house. Langston could buy only the cheapest seats in the upper balcony, but he didn't care.

Between chances to see shows, Langston borrowed plays from the library and read them. He read all the theater news in the daily paper too. From the papers, he learned that plays were being performed in Chicago all the time, and he envied the people who lived there. *He* wasn't likely to get to Chicago even for a visit. He had more chance of going to Denver, where his mother was living.

His mother had married again. Her new husband's name was Homer Clark. She wrote Langston saying that someday she hoped he could live with them. So far, though, nothing had come of the hope.

Then one day when Langston was thirteen,

another letter from her arrived. This one was postmarked not Denver, but Lincoln, Illinois! Langston opened it excitedly.

Dear Lang:

Homer and I want you to come live with us now. We have room for you here, and I think you would like this town. And guess what! You have a baby brother. His name is Gwyn, but we call him "Kit." Can you guess why?

Love,

Mother

Langston could only guess that "Kit" might be short for "Kitten," but if so, Homer Clark must have given him the nickname. Langston was sure his mother would have preferred the fancier-sounding name. She had always liked romantic novels, and he was willing to bet she'd taken the name "Gwyn" from one of them.

The idea of having a brother appealed to Langston. He thought it would be fun to read to

Kit, and to tell him stories like the ones Gran used to tell.

But it was harder than he had expected to say good-bye to the Reeds. He would miss Auntie Reed's cheerful gospel singing, especially "Lord, I Want to Be a Christian," and "I Want to Be a Flower in God's Garden." He would miss Uncle Reed, who got such pleasure out of simple things like sitting by the wood stove on winter evenings, maybe whittling a little something out of pine wood, maybe just plain sitting, resting his "weary bones."

The Reeds were almost family to Langston now. He hoped he could someday let them know, in some meaningful way, just how grateful he was to them.

4. A Family for Langston

When the train slowed and the conductor shouted: "Lincoln!" Langston's heart began to pound. Would he recognize his mother, whom he'd scarcely seen for seven years? Would he and his stepfather get along, or would Homer Clark resent having another mouth to feed? Langston knew his stepfather had a job as chef in a hotel kitchen. Still—as Uncle Reed once said—being able to cook bacon didn't necessarily mean you could put it on your table.

Langston's mother, stepfather, and his baby brother were all on the platform waiting for him. His mother hugged him, then pushed him to arm's length to look at him.

"Why, you're a young man, Lang!" she cried.

"He sure is!" agreed her husband. He grasped Langston's hand and shook it man-fashion in a way that made Langston like him at once.

In the days that followed, Langston found that his stepfather was a warm, friendly man, easy to get on with. At first, though, Homer Clark's habit of "job-jumping" bothered Langston.

"Why does he do it?" Langston finally dared to ask his mother.

"He gets worn out working in hot kitchens," she explained. "He keeps looking for a job that'll be healthier."

Since Homer Clark always seemed to find work, Langston soon stopped worrying.

In the fall of 1915, he entered the eighth grade in the Lincoln Elementary School. He was one of two Negroes in the class, and at first Langston was wary. He remembered the all white school in Topeka, where a few of the children had teased him and called him names.

Nothing like that happened in Lincoln. His classmates accepted him as one of them. He

stood out from them only because he was such a good student. He felt so much at ease with them, in fact, that when they boasted about their family backgrounds, he did too.

"My people came originally from Africa," he declared. Then, daringly, he added, "Who's to say they weren't kings and queens there?"

It was the first time Langston had given any thought to Africa as the land of his beginnings, but it certainly was not to be the last. World War I was now raging. Any mention of Africa in the war news caught his interest.

Because he knew the other children liked him, Langston was not surprised when he was elected to a class office. Their reason for picking him for class poet, however, did surprise him. They'd heard somewhere that all Negroes were born with a feeling for rhythm. They assumed, therefore, that Langston had been too. Since poetry should have rhythm, they believed he was perfect for the position.

"I'll be class poet," Langston told his eighth grade friends, "but I've got to set you straight about something. All Negroes don't have rhythm, any more than they're all musical. My Uncle Reed, for instance, was strictly a one-note singer."

It never occurred to Langston until later that being class poet meant he might actually have to write a poem. Then one day he was told he'd have to do just that — and read it aloud from the stage on graduation day!

The idea of getting up in front of an audience didn't frighten him. He'd done that before in Sunday School. And he guessed maybe he could write a few lines of poetry, without too much trouble. His mother did, from time to time. Back in Kansas, he remembered, she had read them aloud at the Interstate Literary Society, founded by his grandfather.

But could he write a poem good enough to make the class, his teachers, and his family proud of him? Weren't poets supposed to be inspired? Maybe reading the work of some real poet would help?

The only poems he'd really liked, until now, were Longfellow's *Hiawatha* and a few of Paul

Laurence Dunbar's verses. Maybe, since Dunbar was a celebrated Negro writer, his work would have the kind of rhythm his classmates thought all Negroes had.

Langston reread some Dunbar poems aloud. While the rhythm of the poetry was still with him, Langston sat down to write. Of that effort, he said later:

> ". . . My first poem was about the longest one I ever wrote—sixteen verses. In the first half . . . I said that our school had the finest teachers there ever were. And in the latter half, I said our class was the greatest class ever graduated."

The graduation day audience loudly applauded the poem, and Langston was pleased. He could tell by his mother's face that she was proud of him. He was sure his stepfather would have been, too. Unfortunately, Homer Clark was out of town, job-hunting again.

5. Central High School

A few days after Langston's graduation, Homer Clark wrote that he had found a good job in a steel mill in Cleveland, Ohio, and wanted his family to join him.

Langston was sorry to leave Lincoln, because he had been happy there. Nevertheless, he was excited about moving to such a big city. Cleveland proved to be more exciting than Langston had ever dreamed. It was fast becoming an international city. Drawn by the promise of jobs in the steel mills, people of every race, creed, and color were coming to town. There were Negroes fleeing poverty in the southern United States.

There were Jewish immigrants escaping discrimination in eastern European countries. And there were Irish and Italian laborers too.

Central High School, where Langston went in the fall of 1916, was right in the heart of the neighborhood where most of the foreign-born settled. Their children were Langston's classmates.

For the first time Langston became aware of religious and national differences, but they didn't matter to him. He chose people for friends because he liked them. His best friend in high school was a Polish-Catholic boy.

Langston enjoyed high school where he eagerly took part in activities and held many class and club offices. He was on the track team and he was a lieutenant in the military training corps. His gaiety and sense of humor helped make him very popular.

Yet, for all his extracurricular interests, Langston never neglected his studies. Academically, Central High School had very high standards. Foreign-born parents believed that education was a serious business, and even more important, the teachers were dedicated people.

Langston found himself liking subjects he never had liked before. He discovered that mathematics could be as much fun as any puzzle. He learned that art didn't just happen. It had to follow rules of form and pattern, if it was to have meaning or importance.

Langston's art teacher, Clara Dieke, impressed upon him the value of stick-to-it-iveness.

"You've probably all heard the saying, 'Whatever is worth doing at all, is worth doing well,'" she told his class. "But I like to add advice on how to do it. The only way is to start, and to keep on until you finish."

Langston guessed that was right. Only first you had to be sure that what you started was worth finishing, didn't you?

The quotation Miss Dieke had given was not familiar to him, and he was a little shy about asking her to explain it. So he asked his English teacher, Miss Weimer, instead.

"That's from the Earl of Chesterfield's *Letters*

to His Son," she said. "He wrote a series of them telling his son how he should conduct himself in all the affairs of life."

"When did he write them?" asked Langston. "Recently?"

"In the eighteenth century," Miss Weimer said, "but they're considered to be timeless."

Langston, at seventeen, was a lieutenant in Central High's military training corps.

"You mean, as good advice for boys today as for his son back then?"

"Exactly," said Miss Weimer.

"I'm going to borrow the *Letters* from the library and see for myself," said Langston.

"Good," said his teacher. "After you've read them, I'd like to know what you think."

No one had ever before been interested in his opinion but when he went back to talk with Miss Weimer about the book, he made a discovery that revealed a whole new world to him. Talking to someone didn't have to be just conversation. It could be a meeting of the minds.

After that, he often talked to Miss Weimer about things that puzzled him. For instance, why, if art needed rules of form and pattern, did she assign the "free verse" of Carl Sandburg and Vachel Lindsay to her English classes.

"The Kansas City *Star* says free verse is bad because it doesn't follow any poetic pattern," he said.

"That is one newspaper writer's opinion," Miss Weimer replied. "I happen to disagree.

Free verse isn't formless, even though it lacks regular meter and line length. It relies upon natural speech rhythms of the language, Langston."

Langston thought about that for a moment. "Maybe that writer doesn't care for free verse because it's modern," he suggested. "Maybe he thinks only old things are good."

"Maybe. But free verse isn't new, Langston. It was used in the King James translation of the Bible in the Song of Songs and the Psalms."

Across Langston's mind flashed a picture of his grandmother, reading what she called "the most beautiful poem in the world" aloud:

The Lord is my shepherd; I shall not want.
He maketh me to lie down in green pastures:
He leadeth me beside the still waters.
He restoreth my soul ...

Miss Weimer was right. The psalm didn't have regular meter or line length, but it certainly had rhythm.

"I think I could write free verse," he said.

"Why not try to write some?" suggested his teacher.

With her encouragement, Langston did. He found plenty of things to write about — the steel mills where Homer Clark sweated in the heat of the furnaces, the girls who strolled past him on warm spring days, Carl Sandburg, whom he took as his model.

Of Sandburg's poetry he said:

> Carl Sandburg's poems
> Fall on the white pages of his books
> Like blood-clots of song
> From the wounds of humanity.
> I know a lover of life sings
> When Carl Sandburg sings.
> I know a lover of all the living
> Sings then.

Sandburg became Langston's hero. He longed to lead the kind of life Sandburg had as a youth. Sandburg had traveled as a hobo in the West. He had served in the Spanish-American War. He had been an advertising writer and a political worker. He was a newspaper reporter in 1914, when his poems were first published in *Poetry* magazine.

Miss Weimer urged Langston to send some poems to the school magazine, *The Belfry Owl.* He did, and to his delight they soon appeared in print.

"They look like real poetry!" he exclaimed, and read them over and over.

Life in Central High School had gone along so smoothly, Langston had forgotten that being black wasn't always easy. He was reminded of the fact in the summer when he looked for a job.

He and his white friends had started looking at the same time. His friends were hired almost at once. Langston tramped from place to place answering ads, only to be told, "Sorry, you won't do," over and over again.

He finally found work running a dumb waiter, a small elevator for packages, in a department store. The job was not hard, but it was dull. Fortunately, Langston was allowed to read between calls for service.

That fall, Homer Clark decided that work in the steel mills was too backbreaking. Once again he went away looking for something better. When he didn't return after a time, Langston's mother took Kit and went to Chicago to find work.

"You can stay here or come, just as you like, Lang," she said. "You're old enough to be on your own, I think."

The idea of Chicago was tempting, but Langston didn't want to leave Central High School. He spent the summer in Chicago with his mother and Kit and then returned to Cleveland for the school year. He found a single room where he could stay, in return for doing odd jobs.

He was often lonely. He had grown used to the bustle of family life in the past two years, and he missed it. To keep from thinking how quiet his room was, he wrote poems.

These poems were different from the light verse he'd written the previous year. They were personal and serious, so revealing of his private thoughts that he didn't want to show them to anyone he knew.

Still, he wanted someone to read them, so he decided to send the best ones to New York. He made a list of magazines which printed poetry. Then he mailed some to the magazine at the top of his list.

The first try brought only a form rejection slip. So did the second and third. Only one editor sent him a word of encouragement. The editor did not accept the poems for publication, but he told Langston they had "promise" and urged him to "keep trying."

6. Mexico Again

Langston did not need that editor's comment to make him keep trying. By now he could no more stop writing than he could stop breathing. Poems came to him naturally, sometimes complete in his mind before he ever wrote them down.

He was still reading as much as ever, in French as well as in English. The musical prose of Guy de Maupassant appealed to him and he wrote:

"The soft snow was falling through one of his stories ... all of a sudden one night the beauty and the meaning of the words in which he made the snow fall came to me."

He decided at that moment that someday he

would write short stories too. De Maupassant wrote about what he knew best—Paris and the Parisians. He—Langston—would write about America and American Negroes. He would write about his people.

Langston was wise enough to know he had a lot of living to do before he would be ready.

During Langston's junior year at high school, Homer Clark returned to Cleveland. So did Langston's mother and brother, and he was part of a family again.

He had thought that was what he most wanted, but he discovered he'd been much freer living alone. He was used to making decisions for himself now.

"Don't treat me like a baby!" he finally told his mother.

That spring, 1919, Langston's own father made good his plans of twelve years before. When Carrie Hughes had decided to leave Mexico and return to Kansas, he had permitted her to take Langston with her. But he had said, "When I send for him, you'd better see he comes."

Now, Langston received a letter from Mexico.

"I am going to New York for a few days
on a business trip in June. On the way
back, I will send you a wire to be
ready to meet me as the train comes
through Cleveland. You are to accompany me to Mexico for the summer."

The prospect excited Langston. Mexico!
Mountains and sun and cactus! Horses to ride!
Bullfights to see! What a time he'd have!

He gave hardly a thought to the man who
wanted to take him there — his father.

Langston's father was all his mother could
think about. She cried and told Langston he
couldn't go.

"You're ungrateful to even think of leaving me,
after all I've done for you!" she sobbed.

"It's only for the summer," protested Langston.
"Besides I want to get to know my father!"

Langston knew vaguely that his grandmother
hadn't approved of James Hughes and had been

glad when her daughter divorced him. To Langston, however, he was a romantic figure. He owned a ranch in the mountains, and he also had business interests in Mexico City. He must be a lot richer than most Negroes Langston knew in the United States.

"You won't like him," Langston's mother said bitterly. "Stay here with people who love you. You'll be sorry if you don't!"

But Langston's stepfather took Langston's side. "He has a right to get to know his father," Homer Clark said. "I think he ought to go."

Langston did get on the train with his father, but before they reached Mexico he found out that his mother had been at least partly right. James Hughes was not very likable. Money seemed to be all-important to him. He sneered at poor people, saying they wouldn't be poor if they weren't too lazy to work. Langston knew that wasn't necessarily so. Homer Clark nearly killed himself just trying to provide the bare necessities for his family.

The thing that bothered Langston most was

his father's evident hatred of Negroes. He even hated himself for being black. Langston did understand his father's reasons for living in Mexico, though.

"In Mexico anybody with education can get ahead," his father told him. "If you're smart enough, there's no limit to how high you can climb. No one will try to stop you because of your color. I guess you know what I mean by that, eh, boy?"

And of course, Langston did. He still smarted with resentment of the summer before last, when all his white friends had found jobs easily, while he was told, "Sorry, you won't do."

He was glad he wouldn't be going through that experience again this year. Since he had James Hughes to thank for that, Langston decided he ought to be grateful to his father.

"I hope I can be of some use to you on the ranch, Dad," he said, although he didn't have a very clear idea what a ranch in Mexico would be like.

"I have all the ranch hands I need," his father answered.

Langston soon discovered that James Hughes didn't live on the ranch, anyway. His home was in the town of Toluca, where he was manager of an electric light company. He made frequent trips to Mexico City on other business and also to his ranch, but he never took Langston with him.

Before long, Langston was bored. For something to do, he started helping Maximiliano, the Indian house-boy, with his chores. When James Hughes found out, he was furious.

"My son does not have to do a peasant's work!" he said. "If you're so eager to do something useful, you can study bookkeeping. Everybody ought to know how to account for his money. And if you stick with me, you'll make plenty of it!"

He gave Langston a book on elementary book-keeping and a set of problems.

Langston's heart sank when he saw the problems. At Central High, he had learned to enjoy higher mathematics — algebra and geometry — but he had never been good in arithmetic.

"Seventeen years old, and you can't add yet!"

James Hughes exploded, going over the work Langston had done.

He showed Langston what to do again and again, telling him that he had to acquire a "good business head." Then, as if the urging would work some miracle, he'd add, "Now hurry up and do it right!"

So far as Langston could see, "Hurry up!" was his father's favorite expression. James Hughes wanted everybody to hurry up and finish whatever he was doing and then start on the next task.

To be fair, Langston had to admit that his father practiced what he preached. He had enormous energy and he drove himself from dawn to midnight. What James Hughes did not realize was that not everybody was like him.

"Some of us dance to different music," Langston thought.

At first he really tried to hurry in order to please his father. He hoped that good behavior would earn him time off to see something of Mexico. He longed to see a bull fight in Mexico City, and the ancient pyramids of the Sun and the Moon.

All that his efforts won him were harder and harder problems and, in addition, typewriting exercises. James Hughes didn't seem to know the word "fun."

Langston never even got to see the ranch. Lonely and nervous from trying unsuccessfully to please his father, he became ill.

James Hughes called in a local doctor, but the doctor couldn't find anything wrong. "Better take him to Mexico City, where they have better facilities for testing," the doctor suggested.

So at last Langston did go to Mexico City, but not to a bull fight – to a hospital.

All sorts of tests were taken, but they showed nothing physically wrong. For days Langston just lay miserably in bed.

"Maybe the altitude here doesn't agree with him," the doctors finally suggested. "Better take him some place nearer to sea level."

"I'll send him home," James Hughes said.

The minute Langston heard the decision, he began to feel better. By the time he got home, he was almost himself again.

7. Plans

Langston felt sure the real trouble in Mexico had not been altitude, but nerves. He and his father were so different, they set each other's teeth on edge. The summer hadn't been easy for either of them.

After Langston had had time to think about it, he had to admit something else. The quality he had most resented in his father was one he should have admired. Stick-to-it-iveness was a virtue. Hadn't Miss Dieke tried to impress that on the Central High students with her quotation from Lord Chesterfield?

Hoping that maybe they could get to understand each other better, Langston wrote to his father now and then. Soon, James Hughes began to send him an allowance, and Langston was glad, especially now that he had a girl friend.

Susanna Jones had just come up from the South. She loved to dance and had a red dress that inspired Langston to write a poem:

When Susanna Jones wears red
Her face is like an ancient cameo
Turned brown by the ages

    . . .

When Susanna Jones wears red
A queen from some time-dead Egyptian night
Walks once again.

Langston was writing constantly in his spare moments, and by now he was a fair critic of his own work. He kept one notebook for what he thought of as "real poetry" and another for verses and jingles. Real poetry, he felt, had to come from the heart. Verses — well, they were the kind of thing a person could write to order, as he did in his role as class poet.

During his senior year at Central High, Langston was not only the class poet but also the editor of the yearbook. He was on the student council, too. He was a very important person indeed, looked at with awe by underclassmen.

Only a few of the other seniors were making plans to enter college, because most of them would not have enough money. Langston's teachers said they hoped he was going on with his education. Langston wondered if his father would pay for it.

He knew his mother could not give him any money. She was already saying how glad she'd be when he could go to work and be of help to her. Homer Clark was away again, and she had taken a job as a waitress to make ends meet.

"The teachers think I ought to go to college," Langston finally told her.

"Why?" she demanded. "What good did my college education do me? I don't need a degree to wait on tables!"

There was no answer to that argument, at least none that she'd listen to. So Langston said no more about college until he received a letter from his father, asking him to come to Mexico to discuss his "future plans." Knowing James Hughes, Langston was sure that meant plans for college.

He told his mother about the letter. She made a worse fuss than she had the year before, and now there was no Homer Clark to take Langston's side.

Langston had not forgotten how miserable he had been in Mexico the last time, but he was wiser now. And he was sure he had no chance of going to college unless he went to see his father.

His mother scarcely spoke to him after she heard his decision. Her silence hurt him, but he didn't back down. Too much—his whole future, he was sure—was at stake.

She didn't back down either, not even enough to go to the station to say good-bye. Langston kept hoping to the last that she would come. But the train pulled out, leaving him still lonesome, looking out the window.

He felt very sorry for himself for awhile. Then

he made himself think about all the troubles other people had, and how much better it is to look for the bright side of things. Most Negroes at least tried to keep laughing in spite of everything. That set him to wondering afresh how his father could be ashamed of being black. He should be proud!

As Langston sat thinking, the train began to cross the Mississippi River. The water looked golden in the sunset. Staring at it, Langston remembered how large a part the Mississippi and other rivers had played in the history of Negroes through the ages. He thought of the stories people now dead and gone could tell about the rivers they had known!

"I've known rivers!" Langston whispered.

His pulse quickened as the words of a poem began flowing into his mind. Quickly he reached for a pencil and paper. He knew from experience that, if he didn't write the words down immediately, they might never be captured.

Within a few minutes he had written the poem that has since been printed and reprinted in many anthologies and in many languages. He called it "The Negro Speaks of Rivers."

> I've known rivers:
> I've known rivers ancient as the world
>   and older than the flow of human blood
>   in human veins.
> My soul has grown deep like the rivers.
> I bathed in the Euphrates
>   when dawns were young.
> I built my hut near the Congo
>   and it lulled me to sleep.
> I looked upon the Nile
>   and raised the pyramids above it.
> I heard the singing of the Mississippi
>   when Abe Lincoln went down to
>   New Orleans, and I've seen its muddy
>   bosom turn all golden in the sunset.
> I've known rivers:
> Ancient, dusky rivers.
> My soul has grown deep like the rivers.

Writing of rivers seemed to wash away

Langston's sadness. He began to look forward to his arrival in Mexico. Maybe this year things would be better!

For awhile, Langston's father was friendlier. James Hughes seemed willing to meet Langston half way, so a certain comradeship was possible between father and son.

As before, James Hughes went away on urgent business often, leaving Langston behind. But Langston didn't sit and brood this summer. He spoke German with the new German housekeeper, Spanish with the townspeople. He rode horseback and, when he felt lonesome, wrote poetry. He was content enough, in a melancholy kind of way. But he did wonder when his father would get around to discussing those "future plans."

That time finally came when Langston and his father were riding home through the woods after inspecting a flooded silver mine. It was one of several such abandoned mines near James Hughes' ranch land.

"I'm sure those mines will reopen some day,"

James Hughes told Langston. "When they do, they'll have to be reshafted and barracks will have to be built for the workmen. Know what that would mean?"

Langston nodded. "They'd need lumber, and the closest timber is in these woods of yours. You'd make a lot of money."

"Exactly. But so would you."

"Me? Why?"

"By then, you'll be a mining engineer. I need one in my business. Who would be better than my own son?"

Langston held on to the reins with all his might. So those were his father's plans! Did he really understand his son so little?

"I don't want to be a mining engineer! I want to be a writer!" Langston cried.

His father went on talking as if he hadn't heard. "I want you to go to Switzerland to college, where you can learn three languages at once—French, German, and Italian."

"I'm already learning German," Langston mumbled, but again his father paid no heed.

"After Switzerland, you'll go to an engineering school in Germany. Finally — Mexico, to stay!"

"But why do I have to go to Europe?" said Langston. "Why can't I go to engineering school in the United States?"

His father looked at him as if he weren't very bright. "In Europe they don't care about the color of your skin," he answered.

Langston tried desperately to think of a college in the United States where the same thing might be true. One in New York, maybe, for there were more Negroes there in Harlem than in any other city in the country. What was the college near Harlem — Columbia? Yes!

"At Columbia they don't, either," he said, though he was only guessing that was right. "Would you settle for Columbia, Dad?"

James Hughes didn't condescend to answer.

Once again, he and his son were as far apart as the poles.

8. Weary Blues

With this strangeness between them, Langston wouldn't have been surprised if his father had bought a train ticket and told him to take the next train back to the United States. No mention was made of his leaving, however. Since he had no money of his own, Langston had to stay on in Mexico.

He got away from the house as often as possible. He wandered the streets of Toluca, getting acquainted with the other young people. From them he heard talk of the wonders of Mexico City.

"Come up with me to a bull fight," Tomás, a new friend, suggested.

Langston would have liked nothing better, but James Hughes had even stopped his allowance. He scarcely had two *pesos* to jingle in his pockets.

"I would, if I knew where to get some money," he said.

It had never occurred to anybody that James Hughes' son would want to work, for he certainly didn't need to. Tomás spoke to his father about Langston's problem. The older man offered Langston a fee for teaching Tomás English.

The lessons were such a success, other parents asked Langston to teach their sons and daughters too. When the schools opened, he was offered two regular positions as English instructor.

Now with plenty of pocket money, Langston went to Mexico City almost every weekend. He saw famous Spanish matadors fight in the bull ring, and he joined in the many festivals that celebrated Mexican saints' days. Often he had supper with three ladies who were friends of his father, and afterwards attended church with them.

Langston longed to capture such colorful

scenes on paper. But the words he needed weren't suited to poetry, he discovered. So he began to write prose.

Even in prose he couldn't seem to describe things properly. He tore up page after page.

One essay, a description of Mexican games, and a sketch about Our Lady of Guadalupe, finally satisfied him. He sent them off hopefully to New York, to a magazine called *Crisis*. *Crisis* was published by the National Association for the Advancement of Colored People (N.A.A.C.P.), which had been founded in 1910. One of the organization's aims, Langston knew, was "to encourage the intellectual development of the Negro."

"And I," Langston thought, "could surely use some encouragement!"

The *Crisis* editors had just started a magazine for children, *The Brownie's Book,* and they accepted Langston's pieces for publication in it. Better still, they asked to see more of his work!

Excited by this turn of events, Langston dashed off a couple of what he called "top of my head" verses. In one of them, "Winter Sweetness," he described a candy house he saw in a sweet shop in Toluca:

> This little house is sugar,
> Its roof with snow is piled,
> And from its tiny window
> Peeps a maple-sugar child.

He felt sure children would enjoy the rhymes, but he didn't want the editors to think he couldn't write "real" poetry. So, along with the "top of my head" verses, he sent the poem he had written on the train coming to Mexico: "The Negro Speaks of Rivers."

All three were accepted at once. Such success, Langston guessed, would impress even his father. Maybe it would convince James Hughes that his son really might "get someplace" as a writer!

James Hughes quickly pricked the balloon of Langston's elation. "Did they pay you anything?" he asked.

Neither *The Brownie's Book* nor the *Crisis* paid, but authors received free copies of the magazines, and Langston knew that wasn't the kind of "pay" his father had in mind.

"No," he admitted miserably. He waited nervously for the scornful businessman's reaction.

It didn't come. Instead, his father laid a hand briefly on Langston's shoulder.

"Let me see the magazines when they arrive," he said.

Perhaps the sight of Langston's name in magazines of national circulation pleased his father. Perhaps he only wanted to make sure that his son would have a college education. Whatever the reason, in June 1921 James Hughes agreed to send Langston to Columbia.

As is often the sad case when someone finally gets what he thinks he wants, Langston discovered that Columbia was not right for him at all. The classes were too large. It was hard to make friends. Worst of all, Langston did not find the instructors as interesting as those who had taught him in high school. They failed to make him want to work for them.

Before long he went to classes only when he had nothing else he wanted to do. He spent a large amount of time reading, going to shows and lectures, and just wandering around New York, particularly Harlem.

Harlem was an exciting place in the early 1920's. Marcus Garvey, a native of the British West Indies, had come to New York to start a movement of protest about the treatment of Negroes in the United States. He wanted the Negro peoples of the world to unite and establish a great nation in Africa. His slogan was "Back to Africa," and many people were enthusiastic about the idea.

Langston visited Garvey's Harlem head-quarters, a barnlike building called Liberty Hall. To it came visitors from all over the world, as well as people from Harlem.

Among the Harlemites were other young intellectuals like Langston. One of these, whom he liked instantly, was Countee Cullen. Cullen,

Marcus Garvey, founder
of the "Back to Africa"
movement, urged black
people to unite.

a year younger than Langston, was still a high
school student, but he was already famous in
a small way. One of his poems, "I Have A
Rendezvous with Life," was being read aloud
by teachers to their classes and by ministers
to their congregations!

Countee's father was pastor of the Salem
Methodist Church in Harlem. He and his wife had
adopted Countee at age eleven, and Countee

felt a deep sense of gratitude to them. He was going to attend New York University, where, he told Langston, he was planning to work for "the best grades possible," as a kind of present to his parents.

"I guess the 'Back to Africa' thing doesn't steam you up, then?" Langston said wistfully to Countee.

"Does it you?" Countee asked. "Do you really think Garvey's going to get anywhere with it?"

"I don't know," Langston admitted. "But I have decided one thing. I want to go somewhere —anywhere—except back to Columbia."

At term's end, he wrote his father, saying he just wasn't cut out to be an engineer. Then he set out to see if he could get a job on a ship.

After weeks of discouraging answers, he was offered a berth as mess boy—kitchen helper. He accepted at once, too glad to get a job to ask where the ship was going.

It wasn't going anywhere. The ship was part of a fleet of ships that had served in the war and were now kept anchored in the Hudson River, where they'd be ready if needed again. Small crews were kept on board them to oil the engines and act as watchmen.

Langston was disappointed, but he knew the trap he was in was of his own setting. He decided to make the best of things. And actually things could have been much worse. His shipmates, mostly Swedish and Spanish, were friendly. His work was easy. He had plenty of time to write and to experiment with verse forms.

"The Negro Speaks of Rivers" had been compared by critics to Sandburg's work, and Langston knew that Sandburg had influenced his thinking and always would. But now, the "Back to Africa" talk made him think instead of another poet, Vachel Lindsay. Langston remembered how, while yet in high school, he had enjoyed reciting Lindsay's "The Congo," with its boom, boom, BOOM beat of African drums.

Drummers and other musicians were popular in the nightclubs of Harlem, which Langston had visited. The new music, which was really

Langston's Harlem—people, color, excitement and new ideas in the air.

old, was called jazz. Jazz had grown out of the blues. Blues, in turn, had grown out of Negro spirituals and work songs. In these songs hard-working people like Auntie and Uncle Reed could express their thoughts and their sorrows, tell of their happiness and their grief.

Langston had always been excited by music, and he loved watching musicians play. There was one old piano player in Harlem he had seen recently...

Langston grabbed his pencil and beat out an opening verse.

> Droning a drowsy syncopated tune,
> Rocking back and forth to a mellow croon,
>   I heard a Negro play.
> Down on Lenox Avenue the other night
> By the pale dull pallor of an old gas light
>   He did a lazy sway...
>   He did a lazy sway...

Then, suddenly, in the middle of the poem, Langston put a traditional blues verse, one he'd heard back in Lawrence.

> I got the Weary Blues
> and I can't be satisfied.
> Got the Weary Blues
> And can't be satisfied—
> I ain't happy no mo'
> And I wish that I had died.

When he finished, Langston was excited about

the new form he'd discovered for himself. But he wasn't quite satisfied with the ending of the new poem. He put it away in his suitcase, to let it "cool" until he was ready to work on it again. He would send it to *Crisis* later.

Although Langston wrote no other poems that winter, the staff of *Crisis* was interested in meeting him. When Langston changed the address of his subscription the managing editor realized he was in New York and invited him to lunch. Langston didn't want to go, because he thought he'd be tongue-tied with awe of the *Crisis* people, but he didn't want to refuse, either. He accepted an invitation for the first day he had a leave from the ship.

All of the *Crisis* staff did their best to make him feel at ease, especially the editor-in-chief, W.E.B. DuBois. Langston was thrilled to meet the well-known writer, whose famous declaration was often quoted by the young intellectuals of Harlem:

"I am a Negro and I glory in the name. I am proud of the black blood that flows in my veins."

DuBois congratulated Langston on the recent pieces he'd written for *Crisis*.

"You're trying to show our people as they are," DuBois said. "Too many Negro writers pass over their own experiences, to write instead about things they imagine. The only thing that matters, Mr. Hughes, is who and what you are and where you stand. Never shrink from the truth!"

"I'll try not to, sir," said Langston solemnly.

He was now even more eager to write about their people — his and DuBois'. But he still didn't think he knew enough to do it the way he wanted to. He still hadn't lived enough.

"And I won't, if I don't get away from this 'going nowhere' ship," he told himself. "So I'd better start hunting for a job on another one."

9. Launched on a Career

Langston signed on a freighter, the *S.S. Malone*, headed for Africa. He was sure that in Africa he'd feel instantly at home. As long ago as his grammar school days he had boasted about "his people" having come from there.

Langston felt that Marcus Garvey's movement and belief that all blacks should return to Africa was not sensible. Yet the idea fired Langston's desire to see Africa for himself.

The voyage was slow, and by the time the African coastline came into view, Langston could hardly wait to go ashore. He pressed against the railing as the ship nosed toward its pier.

In his mind he cried out to the people he saw:

I am a Negro;
Black as the night is black,
Black like the depths of my Africa.

The "I" he was thinking about, like the "I" in the "Negro Speaks of Rivers," referred not just to him but the whole black race. What he was expressing was pride — pride in his color, pride in his African heritage.

When at last he could go ashore and mingle with the people on land, they snubbed him. He was bewildered. Why was he being treated so?

"I'm black, like you," he cried, "even though I do come from America."

"You're not black," they replied. "No black man has skin the color of copper. You're white."

Langston was shocked by their rejection. To be sure, his skin was not black like theirs. At least one of his ancestors had been Indian. He had some "white" blood too. But he was black. He *was*.

The Africans never did accept him as one of them. And they could not forget that he was American. They resented the arrival of the S.S. *Malone*.

"White men come to take our palm oil and our ivory, our ebony and mahogany," they complained.

Langston, knowing this was true, could only feel sad.

But if his reception by the African people was not as he had dreamed, Africa itself was infinitely more beautiful than he had thought possible. It was:

> "Soft winds, flaming sunsets, the rattle
> of palm leaves, the distant beat of obea
> drums in the night, the surf booming
> restlessly on a sandy beach, and the
> ships from the white man's land
> anchored with lights aglow offshore
> in the starry darkness..."

Langston knew he would never forget Africa.

After his African experience, Langston signed on a freighter going to Holland, and made several New York-Rotterdam round trips. He grew to admire the regular crew members, who seemed to know exactly what they wanted from life. Out of that admiration, too, grew poems. One of them, "Young Sailor," begins:

> He carries
> His own strength
> And his own laughter,
> His own today
> And his own hereafter —
> This strong young sailor
> Of the wide seas.

But that sort of career wasn't for Langston. After several very rough crossings, he decided he'd had enough of seafaring life. The next time his ship touched at Rotterdam, he drew his pay and took the first train going to Paris.

In Paris, Negro entertainers were much in demand, for jazz had taken the country by storm.

Langston couldn't play an instrument or sing, but he managed to get a job as dishwasher in the "Grand Duc," a popular nightclub. Sooner or later, the cream of the Negro musicians then in France would drop in there. Langston, after his work was done, enjoyed listening to the "jam

sessions" that lasted until seven or eight o'clock in the morning. He said,

> "They'd just get together and the music would be on.... They'd weave out music that would almost make your heart stand still...."

Both the hours he worked and the excitement of being a part of the after-hours jazz world made a "night person" out of Langston. When he finally got back to his room, he was often too excited to sleep. So he wrote poems, trying to capture the flavor of what he was experiencing. He wasn't too happy with most of what he wrote, and he guessed why. He was too content with life in Paris.

> "My best poems were all written when I felt the worst. When I was happy, I didn't write anything."

The "Grand Duc's" popularity waned with the

rise of newer clubs, and finally it closed. Langston, out of a job, decided to go back home via Italy.

"Might as well see something of Europe while I'm here," he said.

By the time he reached New York again, in November 1924, he had exactly 25 cents in his pockets. That quarter and a batch of poems were the only assets he had in the world.

For Langston at that moment, they were enough. All he wanted to do now was to get to Harlem and show his poems to Countee Cullen. And a nickel was all the subway ride would cost.

Countee was attending college, but he was also enjoying great success as a poet. Within a space of seven months, his work had been published in eight of the country's leading magazines, including two whole pages in *Poetry*.

Countee greeted Langston enthusiastically, saying he'd arrived at the luckiest possible moment. The N.A.A.C.P. was giving a party that night, and literary people, both black and white, would be there in force.

"You don't need an invitation," Countee

assured Langston. "The fact that you write for *Crisis* is all the passport you'll need."

All the *Crisis* editors were at the party. They told Langston they'd begun to pay writers and that he had earned $20. The news made Langston so happy, he didn't even get tongue-tied when he was introduced to the famous poet, James Weldon Johnson, author of the so-called "Negro national anthem."

Langston pumped the older man's hand enthusiastically. "I think 'Lift Every Voice and Sing!' is just great!" he said.

Johnson smiled at Langston's praise. "I thank you," he said. Then, taking both Langston and Countee by the arm, he led them up to the white writer and literary critic, Carl Van Vechten.

"Carl, here are a couple of gifted young poets I think you'll want to know," Johnson said, introducing them.

"I already know your 'I Have a Rendezvous with Life,' Mr. Cullen," Van Vechten told Countee. "What else have you done?"

He quizzed both Countee and Langston with

Countee Cullen—fellow-poet and friend.

obvious interest. Langston was almost ashamed to admit he'd had fewer poems published than Countee, since he was the older.

"I wonder if I'd be farther ahead if I'd stayed in college," Langston asked himself later. Then, with his usual honesty, he admitted that he couldn't regret his past year's experiences.

A few days later, Langston was the guest of honor at another much smaller party. A group of friends wanted to hear the poems he'd written abroad.

To that party, Countee brought a newcomer to Harlem, a quiet young teacher named Arna Bontemps.

"Arna's a writer, too, Lang," Countee said. "He turned up at my house the other night with a letter of introduction to me. My father opened the door and shouted: 'It's Langston Hughes, Countee!' I don't think you two look much alike, but Dad does!"

"Don't know whether you ought to feel complimented or not, Arna," said Langston, shaking the other's hand, "but I do!"

They all laughed. Then, Langston took Arna around to introduce him.

Langston was tempted to settle down in Harlem, but he felt he ought to go to Washington, D.C. His mother had separated again from Homer Clark and was living in the capital with well-to-do cousins. They were descendants of John Mercer Langston who had been important while Rutherford Hayes was President.

Langston didn't like the idea of being a "poor relation," but maybe rich relatives would help him get a good job. He was twenty-two years old now, and it was time he stopped wandering. Besides, if he could earn enough money, he wanted to go back to college. Howard University was close by. Langston thought that a knowledge of history, sociology, and psychology would make him a better writer.

He soon found that living with the Langstons was out of the question. They were happy to have him because he'd had some success as a writer. But they treated his mother and his nine-year-old brother unkindly.

"We'll find a place of our own," Langston told his mother one day. "With both of us working, we ought to be able to manage."

It was just as hard for Negroes to get good jobs in Washington as anywhere else. Langston was working in a laundry and his mother took a job as a maid. Together they managed to pay for two small unheated rooms.

Whenever he could, Langston put aside a dollar a week toward college tuition. Unfortunately, every time he had a little money saved, it had to

Langston worked hard at a variety of jobs to support his mother and Kit in Washington. For a time he was a busboy.

be spent for things like school supplies or shoes for Kit. Langston got more and more discouraged about his chances of going to college. He was discouraged about Kit, too, for the little boy paid scant attention to his studies.

Between his dislike of his dull job and his worry about the future, Langston was unhappy most of the time he was in Washington. The only thing he enjoyed there were the hours he spent on Seventh Street, the heart of the Negro district. There he heard the kind of rhythms he'd so enjoyed in Cleveland and in Harlem — the blues and shouts of ordinary people, the gospel songs and the jazz. They reminded him of the poem he'd written on board ship — the poem with the unsatisfactory ending, "The Weary Blues."

It was one of the few poems he'd worked over and over unsuccessfully in Europe. Now the infectious rhythms of Seventh Street inspired him to try once more.

This time he was satisfied, so he decided to enter the poem in *Opportunity* magazine's first literary contest. *Opportunity* was published by the National Urban League, an organization formed to improve living conditions for Negroes in big cities.

"The Weary Blues" won the $40 first prize. Langston was invited to the Award Banquet in New York. In order to get there, he had to borrow money, using as security the prize he was to receive.

He sat at the speaker's table with the other award winners, among them Countee Cullen. James Weldon Johnson, the chairman, read Langston's poem aloud.

After reading, Johnson commented on the poem. He said that Langston had chosen the perfect form for saying what he wanted to say.

"The blues form is simple, but just right for expressing the laments of folk Negroes. It speaks the language of the common man, gives just the right mixture of happiness and grief."

When all the speeches were over, many guests

congratulated Langston. Among them was Carl Van Vechten, the white critic Langston had met the year before at the N.A.A.C.P. party.

This time, Van Vechten asked Langston if he had enough poems to fill a book. If so, he wanted to see them.

"If they're as good as 'The Weary Blues,' I think a publisher should be interested," Van Vechten explained.

As soon as Langston got back to Washington, he mailed Van Vechten his poems. Van Vechten sent them on to his own publisher, Alfred A. Knopf, Inc.

In May 1925, Langston received a personal letter from Blanche Knopf. She said Knopf wanted to publish Langston's "delightful" verse.

Langston wrote the good news to Carl Van Vechten.

"I'll always think of 'The Weary Blues' as my lucky poem," he confided.

In answer, Van Vechten suggested that Langston use "The Weary Blues" as the title of his book.

10. Not Without Laughter

When the news of Langston's successes reached Washington, he was invited to a party at the home of an attractive Negro poet, Georgia Douglas Johnson.

"I had no idea you were in the city, Mr. Hughes," she said. "I hold open house for writers every Saturday night. I hope you will drop in whenever you're free."

The evening was the sort Langston liked best. People came by to sip wine and nibble cake, but mainly to talk about poetry and books and plays, and occasionally about jazz.

A fellow guest that first evening was Alain Locke, whom Langston had met in Paris. They'd had lunch together there, and Locke had taken some of Langston's poems. He wanted to consider them for possible use in a special issue about Negro life, which the magazine *Survey Graphic* had asked him to prepare. Now, Locke greeted Langston warmly. "Have you received your copy of the newest *Survey Graphic* yet, Mr. Hughes?" he asked.

"With my poems in it?" asked Langston excitedly.

"Of course," said Locke, and turning to the other guests, he suggested they get and read the magazine too.

In the days to follow, Langston's poems appeared in more and more magazines. Before long, Langston had risen from being an almost unknown contributor to Negro journals to being a nationally respected poet and author.

At Van Vechten's suggestion, Langston occasionally tried his hand at essays too. One essay, "The Fascination of Cities," won second prize in a contest run by *Crisis*. In it, he described his delight in the sounds and smells and sights

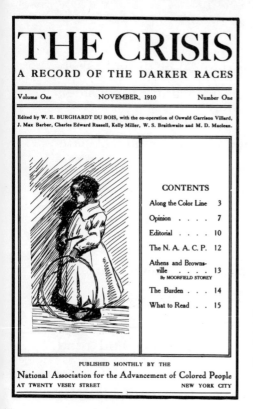

THE CRISIS

A RECORD OF THE DARKER RACES

Volume One — NOVEMBER, 1910 — Number One

Edited by W. E. BURGHARDT DU BOIS, with the co-operation of Oswald Garrison Villard, J. Max Barber, Charles Edward Russell, Kelly Miller, W. S. Braithwaite and M. D. Maclean.

CONTENTS

Along the Color Line   3

Opinion   7

Editorial   10

The N. A. A. C. P.   12

Athens and Brownsville   13
By MOORFIELD STOREY

The Burden . . .   14

What to Read . .   15

PUBLISHED MONTHLY BY THE
National Association for the Advancement of Colored People
AT TWENTY VESEY STREET   NEW YORK CITY

Crisis published many of Langston's early poems. This is the cover of the magazine's first issue.

of the different cities he had visited in the United States, Mexico, Europe, and Africa.

Langston had also entered the poetry contest, but had come in third after his friends Countee Cullen and Frank Horne. The poems he had submitted, "Minstrel Man," and "Cross," were part of his effort to show the real Negro. Both used themes he was to repeat often.

"'Minstrel Man,'" he explained, "emphasized the presence of tragedy behind the Negro's smiling mask."

> Because my mouth
> Is wide with laughter
> You do not hear
> My inner cry?
> Because my feet
> Are gay with dancing
> You do not know
> I die?

"Cross" dealt with the problem of mixed blood, one he later enlarged upon in his play *Mulatto*, a number of short stories, and other poems, too.

Langston's poems for *Crisis* fitted into what was being called the New Poetry Movement. Harriet Monroe, the founder of *Poetry* magazine, was supporting the movement. She had been the first to recognize Carl Sandburg's ability. She had praised "Chicago," one of his first published poems, for being "real and immediate." It described Chicago as the rough, big-shouldered yet proud city it was.

"That's the way poetry should be," she had said then and continued to believe. "Simple and powerful and of *right now*."

Harriet Monroe became interested in Langston's poems and accepted some of his work for her magazine. When he received his author's copy, he leafed through it. Suddenly he saw some new poems of Sandburg's and a thrill went through him.

"I never thought I'd see my contributions and his between the covers of the same book!" he exclaimed. "I wish I could tell Miss Weimer!" Langston had never forgotten his Central High School teacher.

While Langston and his friends were excitedly watching their work appear in print, the black race as a whole was coming to more national attention. Plays about Negroes were the vogue on Broadway. The Negro was featured in novels and popular magazines which had previously refused to print stories about Negroes.

Alain Locke, in his preface to the Negro issue of *Survey Graphic* praised the achievement of Langston and the other young contributors and saw in them a "dramatic flowering" of a new race spirit and pride. Several of Langston's poems appeared in that issue. Following the trend to

James Weldon Johnson, dean of Negro writers, inspired Langston and other young black poets.

glorify Africa, in "Dream Variations" he imagined how delightful it would be:

> To fling my arms wide
> In some place in the sun,
> To whirl and to dance
> Till the bright day is done.
> Then rest at cool evening
> Beneath a tall tree,
> While night comes on gently
> Black like me
> That is my dream!

In another poem, he gave his own "battle call" of encouragement for his people:

> We have tomorrow
> Bright before us
> Like a flame
> Yesterday, a night-gone thing
> A sun-down name —

Many people became interested in black

artists and writers at that time. Langston and his friends enjoyed the flattering attention, but they knew they could not count on this interest to last. So Langston was delighted when he was accepted by Lincoln, a Negro college near Philadelphia. He wanted very much to enroll there.

"A friend who's a student there tells me he gets all the free time he needs for experimenting," Langston told Countee.

"That means, I'd be able to keep on with my writing. I'll need to do that in order to support myself."

Then at Christmas, 1925, came an unexpected present. It was a letter from a woman, a patron of the arts, whom he'd met at a party. She had heard that Langston wanted to go to college, and she offered him the money to do so.

He said later, "It was the happiest holiday gift I ever received."

He entered Lincoln in February 1926. He studied hard, but he enjoyed life too. He skated on the village pond with the other boys, played basketball, and went to club meetings and parties.

Hard-working but light-hearted, Langston posed
at Lincoln University for this picture.

Many weekends, he went to Harlem, to keep in touch with his literary friends.

Among these were several new ones, and during his first summer vacation from Lincoln, Langston moved in with one of them. With him and others, Langston created a new magazine called *Fire*.

"Why do you call it that?" Countee asked.

"It's symbolic," said Langston. "We hope it will fire young Negroes into writing what they really want to write."

For *Fire* Langston wrote "Elevator Boy," "Brass Spittoons," and other realistic poems, all of them memorable for their honest portrayals of Negro workmen. All contributions used in the magazine were about ordinary, unglamorous human beings. To Langston's surprise, *Fire* was criticized bitterly by older Negro leaders.

Without support, *Fire* could not live. It died after one issue.

Fine Clothes to the Jew, Langston's second book of verse, was published midway through his college career. Most of the poems in it are based on Negro folk music. Through the medium of blues, street sounds, religious shouts, Langston tried to express how Negroes really felt. In "Porter," for instance:

> I must say
> Yes, sir,
> To you all the time.
> Yes, sir!
> Yes, sir!
> All my days
> Climbing up a great big mountain
> Of yes, sirs!

White reviewers praised the book for its honesty and beauty, saying: "It is hard to praise too highly one who expresses a race's emotions — and a moment in its life. Mr. Hughes has done both."

But Negro reviewers did not like it, for the portraits, like those in Langston's magazine *Fire* were of the poor working people. One reviewer charged: "It does not matter ... whether every poem in the book is true to life. Why should it be paraded before the American public by a Negro author as being typical ... of the Negro?"

"I write about what I know best," Langston replied simply, "as an artist should."

During his last two years at Lincoln, Langston devoted all his free time to writing a novel. *Not Without Laughter* was based on his childhood in Kansas. The characters are a boy, Sandy, his mother, and his wandering romantic father, and include his grandmother and two aunts. The novel tells of Sandy's early experiences with school and work, race and family.

The importance of laughter is stressed throughout the book. It was the same kind of laughter Langston's· grandmother talked about. The sad part of the book, though, was that everybody could laugh except Sandy himself. He did not yet understand why laughter was necessary.

Not Without Laughter's sales quickly surpassed those of Langston's poetry books. It has since been translated into eight languages and has become an international success.

11. Keep Your Hand on the Plow

By the time Langston graduated from college in 1929, the wave of Negro popularity had collapsed. This was partly because people had turned to new interests, but mostly because the country was sliding into a terrible financial depression.

When the stock market crashed in October 1929, New York was especially hard hit. Thousands of businesses failed. Millions of people were out of work.

The situation was discouraging even to someone with a "tomorrow will be better" philosophy like Langston.

Langston went to Cleveland, where his mother and brother were now living and stayed with them for a while. Kit, now fifteen, was attending Central High School, but he didn't find the same interests there that Langston had. The two brothers were not alike.

Out of the blue, Langston got a wonderful surprise. *Not Without Laughter* won the Harmon Gold Award, given annually by the Federated Council of Churches to the book considered "most noteworthy for service in the interests of human welfare." Langston received a gold medal and a $400 check.

He decided to spend the money for a relaxing holiday, and left at once for the island of Haiti.

There he gloried in the sunshine, the music, and the laughter of carefree people. He lay on the sand and tried to puzzle out how he could make a living doing what he wanted to do — writing what he wanted to write.

He said in his book, *I Wonder As I Wander:*

"I did not want to write for the pulps,
or turn out fake 'true' stories. . . . I did
not want to bat out slick non-Negro
short stories. . . . I wanted to write
seriously and as well as I knew how
about the Negro people. . . ."

On his way down to Haiti, he had stopped briefly at Bethune-Cookman College in Daytona Beach, Florida. When the college president, Mary McLeod Bethune, had asked him to read some of his poems to English classes, the students greeted the reading with enthusiasm. Mrs. Bethune had said afterwards: "Why don't you tour the South reading your poems? Thousands of Negro students would be proud and inspired by seeing you and hearing you. You are young, but you have already made a name for yourself in literary circles. You can help black students to feel that a Negro youth can amount to something in this world in spite of our problems."

Langston thought more and more about her suggestion, and the more he thought, the better it sounded to him. The problem was money, for the Harmon Award cash was almost gone.

Langston returned to New York in the fall of 1931. He had heard about the Rosenwald Fund to aid Negro education, so he wrote the trustees a letter outlining his plan. They approved it and sent him $1000.

With part of the money, Langston bought an old car. As he didn't know how to drive, he asked a former Lincoln classmate to accompany him.

"You can be my business manager and share my profits, if you do the driving," Langston said.

"That beats being a red cap in this tipless town," his friend, a part-time baggage carrier at Pennsylvania Station, agreed.

Langston knew in advance that not all the places he wanted to visit could afford to pay him.

His publisher helped by issuing a special one dollar edition of *The Weary Blues*. With that to sell, he was sure he could get along.

That fall and winter he covered every state in

the South. Thousands of Negro students heard and applauded him. "People need poetry," Mrs. Bethune had said, and she was right.

Tight as his schedule was, Langston always found time to help students who wanted to become poets themselves. One student was Margaret Walker. Twelve years later, her first book of poems, *For My People*, received the Yale University Young Poet's Award. When she sent Langston an advance copy, she inscribed it:

"To Langston—in gratitude for his encouragement even when the poems were no good."

Langston talked to audiences of children, too. He was so pleased by the reception they gave him that he decided to put together a book just for them. He selected what he called "pleasant poems" from both *The Weary Blues* and *Fine Clothes to the Jew*. They were poems that painted pictures, like "Mexican Market Woman," "April Rain," and "Winter Moon."

First poetry—then autographs for all!

He often read "Winter Moon" to children:

How thin and sharp
    is the moon tonight!
How thin and sharp and ghostly white
Is the slim curved crook
    of the moon tonight!

Knopf published the book under the title *The Dream Keeper* in 1932.

That same year Langston teamed with Arna Bontemps to write a story for young people, *Popo and Fifina*. It tells of a brother and sister who have to move away from their old home to a new one far away. Its setting is Haiti, and the descriptions of the exotic island are vivid. A reviewer said of the book: "It would be well if all travel stories were written by poets."

Langston ended his speaking tour abruptly in the spring of 1932, when he was offered the chance to go to Russia and help write a film about Negro life. The film was never produced, but Langston welcomed the chance to see Russia. He loved to travel, to meet new people, and to hear new music.

From Russia he traveled to the Far East. He discovered, to his delight, that all of his books were popular there. He was entertained lavishly, particularly in China and Japan.

Langston was away for over a year. During this time he began to write short stories seriously and was excited by the results. In the short story he had found the kind of prose he wrote best.

Langston hadn't realized how much he had missed his native land until his ship sailed into San Francisco Bay. He could hardly wait for the ship to dock. When it did, he went directly to the house of a friend who had been cordial to him during his speaking tour the year before.

Noel Sullivan, a wealthy white man, lived on fashionable Russian Hill. He welcomed Langston warmly and asked him about his experiences and his plans for the future. Langston talked freely and frankly. He ended his recital by confiding his newest dream.

"I want to write enough short stories about my people to fill a book," Langston said.

"Then you'll need peace and quiet," Sullivan answered. "My cottage at Carmel-by-the-Sea is yours for a year, if you want it."

The offer was like a gift from heaven. Langston could settle down and work now without interruption and without worrying about money. Noel Sullivan told no one where Langston was, so few people bothered him and he was able to work 10 to 12 hours a day. When the solitude

At Carmel Langston found the solitude he needed to experiment with new forms of writing.

became too depressing he went to San Francisco to spend an evening talking and enjoying music with his friends.

Langston wrote a great many stories, many of them telling of Negro-white relationships. The first story he wrote, "Cora Unashamed," is also one of his best. Cora, a Negro cook in a white household, dominates the story. She is the kind of American Negro, wise and warm and modest, that Langston characterized in all his most successful work.

"Cora Unashamed" and a few other stories

were accepted by important national magazines, but some editors rejected Langston's work. They said it was no longer profitable to feature Negroes in publications for the general public.

Langston was disappointed, but not discouraged. He had said long ago that black wouldn't seem beautiful forever. But he kept on writing short stories until he had enough to fill a book. Late in 1933 he sent them to Mrs. Knopf, who agreed to publish them under the title *The Ways of White Folks*.

At about the same time, the old Mexico City sisters whom Langston had enjoyed visiting wrote him of his father's death.

Langston felt a pang of loss at the news, even though he had not seen his father since he'd left Mexico for Columbia many years before. He was asked to come to Mexico for the reading of the will and decided to do so although he was sure that James Hughes had not left him any money. As he had expected, he was not mentioned in the will, but Langston enjoyed life in Mexico and decided to spend the winter there.

When he returned to California, he learned that his mother, still in Cleveland, was seriously ill. So, instead of going back to Carmel and his writing, Langston hurried East instead.

His mother's treatment was expensive, and once again Langston was desperate for money. *The Ways of White Folks* was not selling well.

"In depression times like these, people buy bread, not books, Mr. Hughes," a magazine editor told him.

Fortunately for Langston, his play *Mulatto*, written five years earlier, found a producer, and was a success.

While Langston was living with his mother in Ohio, he wrote other plays. They were staged by the Gilpin Players, a group of professional actors, all Negro. *Little Ham*, a Harlem folk comedy, proved to be especially popular with Cleveland audiences. Today it is called a "period piece," because all the talk is related to the 1920's. In spite of that, its characters—Ham, Madam Bell, Lulu and Tiny Lee—are persons much like those on the streets of Harlem today.

Langston enjoyed writing plays about "just folks," as he called his characters. He was grateful to the Gilpin Players for performing them.

"There ought to be a little theater like this in Harlem," he told them. "Maybe I can do something about it."

He wrote about his plans to Blanche Knopf. In the letter he also said that he was considering writing an autobiography. In her reply, Mrs. Knopf encouraged the book idea.

In January, 1937, Langston began to write *The Big Sea.* He had scarcely started when he was asked by the Baltimore *Afro-American* to go abroad to report on the Civil War in Spain.

The invitation made him hesitate. He had always wanted to see Spain, but he was worried that his mother couldn't manage without him. She wouldn't lack for money, for *Mulatto* was bringing in plenty, but she needed someone around to help her.

Kit, whom Langston was supporting through college, came home for spring vacation. He'd been neglecting his work and was close to failing.

"It might be good for you to take a term off and get a job," Langston decided. "Will you stay in Cleveland and look after Mother?"

Kit agreed, and Langston departed for Spain.

He was assigned to write about the Negroes who had come from all over the world to fight on both sides. He said in *I Wonder as I Wander:*

> "Among the things I wanted to find out was what effect, if any, the bringing dark troops to Spain had on the people in regard to their racial attitudes. Had color prejudice been created in a land that had not known it before?"

He found the same answer everywhere. He, a black, was well-received everywhere he went, and so were all the blacks in the International Brigades. There didn't seem to be the slightest tinge of color prejudice in Spain.

Death was a constant companion for everyone, for people who had come to Spain to take part in the war, as well as for people who lived there. What impressed Langston was their bravery.

"The will to laugh . . . under fire, each
person in constant danger, was to me
a source of amazement."

Langston returned to the United States in the winter of 1938. He found that Kit had gone back to college, leaving neighbors to "look in on" his mother. So Langston settled down in Cleveland once again.

There he finished *The Big Sea*. It was published by Knopf in 1940 and was a great success. One critic said:

"This is a moving, worthwhile book . . .
a most valuable contribution to the
struggle of the Negro for life and
justice and freedom and intellectual
liberty in America."

Langston's mother died at about the same time

Langston Hughes at work in his study

the United States entered World War II. After her death Langston moved to an apartment in Harlem, but he couldn't spend much time there during the war. As his contribution to the war effort, Langston wrote patriotic radio plays, urging people to buy war bonds and to give blood to blood banks. He also traveled coast to coast, giving poetry readings and lectures to soldiers in U.S.O. centers. His most popular talks were about the latest jazz style, "boogie," and the bands and singers that were making it famous. He used a phonograph and played records as background music while he read. His voice

The poet takes his poetry to the air waves.

rose and fell with the accompaniment, almost as if it too were a musical instrument.

The servicemen listened and applauded.

"You should have been an actor," they said.

"If I were, I wouldn't have *me* to write the things I'd want to act," he joked in answer.

During the war, Langston wrote no poetry or prose of protest. Life was grim enough for everybody, and he felt people deserved light entertainment — "upbeat" material.

Langston's *Shakespeare in Harlem,* was certainly that. Most of the poems in it were based on jazz rhythms or "sweet-sad" blues. It was verse that was meant to be "read aloud, crooned, shouted, recited, or sung." "Love," for one, was set to music.

> Love is a wild wonder
> And stars that sing,
> Rocks that burst asunder
> And mountains that take wing.

Langston wrote some patriotic poems too.

One of them, "Freedom's Plow," was read to radio audiences by the dramatic actor, Paul Muni. He was accompanied, at Langston's special wish, by an organ and four male singers. The refrain is:

"KEEP YOUR HAND ON THE PLOW!
    HOLD ON!"

In 1943, Langston went back to Lincoln University to receive the honorary degree, Doctor of Letters. The moment when the colorful academic hood was slipped over his head was one of the proudest of his life.

12. Poet of His People

Langston was glad to have his Harlem apartment for home base.

"My favorite people live in Harlem," he said.

He didn't mean only his literary friends, though they were delighted to have him around. He meant *his* people. The people he'd promised to portray as they really were.

He kept this promise faithfully by creating his most popular character: Mr. Jess B. Semple of Harlem, U.S.A., nicknamed "Simple."

Simple first appeared on November 21, 1942,

in a Negro newspaper, The Chicago *Defender*, to which Langston contributed occasionally.

Simple was an instant hit, and readers clamored to hear more about him. They liked him because he was "just folks." The things that happened to him could have happened to anybody in Harlem — or any other place.

Langston's neighbors were Simple's people

Critics, both black and white, agreed with the readers. Apparently, the old ideas about the need to romanticize the Negro had disappeared.

Simple, however believable and lovable, is, nevertheless, a symbol. He is the living example of Langston Hughes' favorite theme. He is a Negro; he's proud to be black; he is scornful of anyone who does not share his pride.

Langston stressed this theme over and over again in the five books he filled with Simple's adventures. One clear example is in the prize-winning *Simple Takes A Wife*.

"Some colored folks are ashamed to like watermelon. I told you about that woman who bought one in the store and made the clerk wrap it up before she would carry it home.... Me, I would carry a watermelon unwrapped any day anywhere. I would eat one before the Queen of England."

The poetry Langston wrote now was mostly

gay and humorous. "Fun stuff," he called it, reading it aloud to his friends. Even the poems that had serious themes he brightened with upbeat endings:

Though you may hear me holler,
And you may see me cry—
I'll be dogged, sweet baby,
If you gonna see me die.
Life is fine!
Fine as wine!
Life is fine!

Langston was finding life fine, though he kept peculiar hours. "I'm a night person," he said. "Have been ever since my Paris days."

His friends knew that. They also knew they were welcome in his home any time and any evening. Even if he wasn't home, they knew where to find the key. Often he'd return from the theater to find them listening to his records or heatedly discussing some topic. He'd join them, and the talk would go on for the entire night.

After they'd left, Langston would sit down to write.

"Can't work when I'm rested," he said with his usual dry humor.

He was writing for the theater as well as attending it. He was particularly interested now in plays with musical accompaniment. His gospel scenes were enlivened with the singing of spirituals. His Harlem scenes were made real with street calls and bursts of jazz.

In 1947, Langston wrote the lyrics for a musical version of Elmer Rice's play, *Street Scene*. At the time, he was at Atlanta University where he had accepted a one year Visiting Professorship.

He enjoyed that teaching job enough to accept another the following year. This time he was Poet-in-Residence at the Laboratory School of the University of Chicago. In Chicago he continued to write plays. These were acted by the Skyloft Players, a Negro Theatre group he had founded during the war.

Langston's young students at the Laboratory School were a bright group of teenagers. For them he brought to life thrilling chapters of American history. Using his flare for acting, he made them "see" the black heroes of America.

He did the same for famous Negro musicians. Occasionally he even brought some real ones to class with him.

"Here's the Duke," he'd say, introducing Duke Ellington, a personal friend.

When he didn't have the "real thing," Langston would enliven his talks with records from his huge collection. It included all sorts of music, from gospel "shouts" to "be-bop." He never left home for long without his records.

"I'd rather live without food than without music," he said.

The lectures Langston gave in Chicago were later edited and published in books for all young people to read. They are lively reading, even without musical accompaniment.

After two years of teaching, Langston returned to spend nearly all of his time in Harlem.

"I like to be where people can find me," he said, his eyes twinkling.

At home—in Harlem—in New York

His friends were quick to hear the humor underlying his words.

"Sure," they said. "That's why you never got to travel around the world."

He had his fingers in too many pies to get away easily now. He wrote poetry and prose. He finished a second volume of his autobiography. He translated the work of several Spanish and French authors into English. He did a history of

Langston surrounded by his friends

the N.A.A.C.P. and edited several anthologies of Negro poetry and prose. One of the latter he did with his old friend, Arna Bontemps.

In everything he did, Langston's aim was the same. He hoped to show how the black American feels and what he wants. He tried to do it with understanding, humor, and optimism.

This aim was recognized and rewarded over and over again. In 1953, *Simple Takes A Wife* received the Ainsfeld-Wolfe Award as the best book of the year on race relations. In 1960, Langston won the Spingarn Medal, awarded annually to a Negro of outstanding achievement.

Through all this, Langston kept himself where people could find him. And they came in great numbers. The great of the literary and jazz world came. So did the would-be-great, for Langston was never too busy to encourage young writers. He had never married, and these young people were as dear to him as the children he'd never had.

"Whenever I see one of you publish," he said, "it's like seeing myself in print for the first time."

Langston collected the poems of these young writers until he had enough good ones for a book. Indiana University published it as *New Negro Poets U.S.A.* in 1964.

The last three years of Langston's life were as busy as his youth. A month before he died, he made a trip abroad to talk about his latest Simple book, *Simple's Uncle Sam.*

Langston Hughes lived long enough to see his *Black Nativity* produced all over the world.

His death in New York on May 22, 1967, came unexpectedly after a short illness. The next day, the news was carried on the front page of the *New York Times*. For days afterwards letters from people who had loved him and tributes from all the national Negro organizations were printed in that newspaper.

Vinnette Carroll, producer of Langston's gospel-song play, *Black Nativity*, spoke for the many people Langston had helped toward success.

> "Growing up, I was fed and inspired by Langston Hughes' poetry. In my maturity, he gave not only to me, but to countless Negroes, a chance to experiment and expand...a chance to be just a little bit better than we had dreamed possible."

Langston Hughes had truly become a "poet of his people."

Index

142

143